Young of the Year

Young of the Year

Sydney Lea

Four Way Books
Tribeca

for Creston Wade, Ivy Carola, Cora Jane, and Arthur Epperson, and for their mothers and fathers.

Holy! Holy! Holy! Holy!
All of heaven came to sing!
Behold a miracle . . . .

Please direct all inquiries to:
Editorial Office
Four Way Books
POB 535, Village Station
New York, NY 10014
www.fourwaybooks.com

Library of Congress Cataloging-in-Publication Data

Lea, Sydney, 1942-
    Young of the year : poems / by Sydney Lea.
        p. cm.
    ISBN 978-1-935536-10-9 (pbk. : alk. paper)
    I. Title.
    PS3562.E16Y68 2011
    811'.54--dc22

                                    2010032298

This book is manufactured in the United States of America
and printed on acid-free paper.

Four Way Books is a not-for-profit literary press. We are grateful for the assistance
we receive from individual donors, public arts agencies, and private foundations.

This publication is made possible with public funds
from the National Endowment for the Arts

and from the New York State Council on the Arts, a state agency.

NYSCA

Distributed by University Press of New England
One Court Street, Lebanon, NH 03766

[clmp]   We are a proud member of the Council of Literary Magazines and Presses.

CONTENTS

I. Mercy, Mercy, Mercy

II. Neighbors

III. Birds, a Farrago

IV. Dispute with Thomas Hardy

I. Mercy, Mercy, Mercy

BENT TREE, STRAIGHT SHADOW

The skeletal Mr. Bloch flunked me in physics.
He gathered some courage and told me I'd never tried.
What if I had?
        I'd still have been mystified.
Something always goes wrong between me and numbers.
The thing that stopped me dead in my tracks, for instance,
on the northside slope of Checkerberry Knoll,
at three o'clock today, in January,

Vermont, 2008—the thing I saw
would all add up for one whose mind's behavior
was different from mine,
        but I stood still in wonder
while the scurfy trunk of a half-dead sugar maple
got struck somehow by the unobstructed sun
and showed a shadow straight as string on the snow.
I couldn't make it make sense. Bent tree, straight shadow.

Would some equation explain it? Maybe, but not
my thinking, which flew off anyway but straight.
To Bloch, as it happened:
        blackboard-chalked cheap suit,
oversized and wrinkled like animal skin.
Haywire hair. An expression between pure rage
and pain as our pack of brutish adolescents—
all in a circle, dreaming up jibes so sharp

we'd dream they drew blood—jeered the hopeless teacher.
None of us wanted to grow up Mr. Bloch.

Neither did Bloch,
            I'd bet. So if when you talk
of the young you grow lyric, you've never known a child
or never *been* one. It takes a lifetime, it seems,
to have a heart, to make certain things add up.
I wondered whether the man still strode this earth.

Cold snow chirped underfoot as I strode along
in search of more legible signs. Dark blood and hair
and frozen dung
                said the deer gave the neck just there.
It was easy to figure: the pack of coyotes circling,
the kill, the parts all dragged downhill and up.
When I arrived, there was nothing else remaining
besides that blood, the shitballs, the scattered hairclumps.

The backbone, the hooves,
            the very hide—all missing.

ANOTHER BREAKUP

—at the House of Chan

He reaches back for his wallet, bloated with snapshots of vanished women,
of children who rarely phone, and he thinks: *I sure could use some luck.*
He could sure have done some things. Or better, left a few undone:

sneering at poor Eileen, for instance, for dimples at stocking's top
or Veronica for that metal scritch in her voice—as if his own
were some famous tenor's, his body so splendid it belonged in a men's magazine.

He laments some words he slung like mud. They've driven off yet another.
He rues devouring whatever it was just now with that sauce that singed
his blood. *I burn,* he breathes, comparing great things with small. He winces:

the women all hated that habit. He wishes the tears that stand on his cheeks
could stand for an inner and spiritual . . . so on. *In lust I burn.* It isn't
so much his mind's pornography he curses here in silence

as this grandiosity that always turns his circumstances
ugly as cuttlefish warts. *I might as well have eaten bugs,*
he says to himself, now that the eating's over. Still he savored it all,

each brutal bite, for which he atones with purging belches—polite,
he's heard or read somewhere, in distant Asia, a world that's likely
otherwise refined beyond his gross imagination.

Or so he imagines. He lusts. For something. Even superstition.
Cracking the cookie's carapace, he unfolds and reads the fortune:
A man should turn to serener thoughts at the end of a muddy season.

He wants a hopeful metaphor, like some gorgeous thing burst out
of a springtime chrysalis composed of insect-spit and -dung.
He repeats the saying, rises, pushes out through the beaded curtain.

RAIN

—in honor of Clifford Brown

December. It shouldn't be raining.
Damn a rain in winter.
Bent fieldgrass seems to suffer
under wet snow it's holding.

Woodsmoke's flat on the trees,
there's rain, and the good die young.
So they say. And I? I got born
too much later. What was the year

he last jammed at Music City
just two hours from me down in Philly—
'56 or '55?
What difference? I was alive,

but only twelve or thirteen
when he cut those bootleg discs.
Freddie Powell, his piano man,
got killed when his Buick flipped

that night in the rain, and his wife
as well, who'd been driving, and Clifford.
My untextured town despised
a certain disheveled neighbor.

I liked him. He'd spun me a record—
Art Blakey's *A Night at Birdland*—
with a man named Brown on trumpet.
I know of course it's worthless

to say I felt magic—and pain.
It seems so naive today,
my vow to myself that I'd see him.
(In my dreams I wished I could *be* him.)

One day I'd see Clifford Brown,
who by now would be damned near eighty
as I speed down this fast lane from sixty
just sitting here at home.

Testy old crank I've become,
I curse the rain of an evening
fifty long years gone.
I hear the *thwack-thwack* and humming

of windshield wipers, the *thrip*
at each pavement seam, a hiss
of an evil wet flying up
off the tires. Nancy says *Shit*

behind the wheel, then quiets.
Brownie don't go for cursing.
I hear it all as I'm spinning
"Joy-Spring," reviling that night.

Unjoyful, I curse it all:
how the rain that shouldn't rain
keeps thumping down, how an owl
coasts quiet through the dark of the day

into woods intending to strike
something dead in the damp. I wish
I'd heard Clifford perform "Brownie Speaks."
I'm a fool, I have to admit—

I yearn to tinker with time,
put a magic spell on the rain,
blow it away and gone.
Rain—all gone. And pain.

THE 1950S

The boys went back and forth between scamming and snubbing
the girl who showed up late afternoons to watch
each practice and game, her elbows propped on the boards
as their bodies flew by. Cinder block and I-beam
echoed with grunts and the claps of sticks on pucks.

Before they showered, unlacing skates on the bench,
they threw fingers to see who'd be the one to go find her.
They bragged about what they'd make her do, or had.
Some of them must have known her actual name,
so there's no excusing what the young punks called her:

among themselves, the girl was always *Rink-Rat*.
Where was the school where Rink-Rat took her classes?
Nobody cared, or wondered how her family—
if she had a family, that is—could set her free
to hang around with boys at play, and after.

Behind the building, a path of mud and cinders
snaked past propane tanks and garbage cans
up a squat little hill that was more or less out of sight.
Not exactly a bower, but atmosphere wasn't the issue
in the dead of winter, when it all had to be quick fun.

Much later, driving past some stark cold scene
that sketchily resembles that meeting place,
one of the boys, who may now be a father to daughters,
shivers, thinking back on a blurry figure
with bottle-thick glasses lopsided on her face—

her savagely birth-marked face. The mark is what lingers
more than anything. It started under an ear,
as they saw when she wore her limp hair up or in braids.
She tried out other styles too. The boys didn't care,
her body was all that mattered. As one of them sneered,

The chassis's not half bad, as though if she weren't a rodent,
she could be a machine. What was the desperate longing,
if that's what you'd call it, that made her so easy a mark?
Why on earth would she come and come and come?
Oh they had some fun with that word, their double-meanings

as lame as each of them was surely mistaken.
The rink-rat-machine would thrash and sigh and moan,
a pretense the graceless boys didn't bother with.
Her birth-splotch took the nastiest possible path:
from that ear to the edge of her scalp and straight back down,

turning her oversized nose, all acne and blackhead,
to a blob of berry and paste and melting chocolate,
her chin the same. So the boys were playing two games,
one with nets and goalies, the other with Rink-Rat.
After their sweat cooled down, they talked about hockey:

they praised their own teamwork, deception, brotherhood, speed.
In short they swapped the mindless swaggerer's claims
that men have always shared.
                                    I'm saying *they,*
you'll understand, as I try to skate over shame
it seems to have taken me all these years to name.

SLOW BURN

She writes to him after this lifetime of silence.
There's a tumor. *They tell me it's final.*
She adds, *My father's farm burned down.*
       Oh no no no.
           First love meant hot vinyl
all through one summer. They crooned
along with that Platters tune

they treasured: *Smoke Gets in Your Eyes.*
Long drought, but they felt exalted by sighs:
for children like them hot love meant salvation—
       but no. Oh no.
           There's a beech tree, or was:
are they still there, his incisions
in its trunk? Their crude initials . . .

Her treatment failed, having *charred the innards.*
How quaint, her diction. Fat clouds gathered,
he vaguely recalls—as they lay in thrall
       to their radio—
           over thirsty acres.
Rain threatened but never fell.
She wants *to catch up, that's all.*

Later she'd have a son and daughter,
who in mind dashed through some suburb's sprinklers.
They must look like each other, would not be taken
       for his children. No.
           He imagines specters:

gap-beaked turkeys shaking
dry wattles, mute geese scolding,

and her late old man's late cows and heifers
inaudibly bawling in stalls of cinder.
Absence, silence. After some brief season—
            what can he do?—
                  her disaster will kill her.
Both adults, the children.
Perhaps that's consolation.

He and she scarcely noticed dead leaves
and corn in the fields, wizened at seed.

MEN WITHOUT WOMEN

I turned a corner in Montreal
right after the poor stiff went down,
the one who'd hit him having proved himself
The Better Man, and showing
that almost sexual victory face,
all heavy lid and smirk.
I wasn't scared, I wasn't angry,
I couldn't know after all
what had started this mess. It was something else,
the look in the light-colored eyes
of the fallen one—down on his knees
and not about to get up—
that quickened my step and made me wish
I could close my own eyes now
and still make my way along the sidewalk.
I didn't like how the victim
appeared to be knocked way back to his childhood—
no hint left of swagger,

just boyish confusion in those milk-blue eyes,
eyes that might start leaking
at any moment now, I feared.
I understand what I say
may be so much hairy-chested horseshit,
and yet I understand too
how bitter and hard it can be on a man
to be shown up like that. I recall,
all but five full decades ago,
stepping outside from a club
where Clyde McPhatter had ended his set,

and how full I felt of that wail
and whisper and funk, how I saw the stars
winking down from between tall buildings,
everything right with the world except
I had no lady-love.
The shore-leave sailor lurched my way,
a scrawny little bastard,

but drunk enough to be rhino-sized
and growing. He shoved me hard,
or hard as he could manage, perhaps
because I happened to be
the only other young man there
on that sidewalk, by that door.
He called me Ralph. "Hey, you ain't foolin'
around with no baby, Ralph."
As if I were the one who'd started the fooling.
I straightened, stared him away,
and turned to go. His wheelhouse swing
grazed my ear from behind,
completely painless, but it got me crazy:
I had only wanted to love
the way I was feeling and was only wishing
some woman could feel it with me.
My punch didn't miss. Down on his knees,
the poor jerk shook his head

and hacked, the fist I'd thrown having caught him
not on the chin but under,
right on the Adam's apple. Kneeling,

he started to cry out loud,
his skinny chest rising and falling so
he looked—well, he looked like a baby,
complete with sailor suit, complete
with that harmless gaze of confusion
in his eyes, light blue like eyes just now
on a street in a Canada city,
miles and miles from that club yet close
as close can know. And so:
I bent and helped my sailor up
and brushed him clean and walked off.
All this as I remember went down
after Clyde had left the Drifters.
But it was, I think, before he recorded
the aching *Without Love*.

MERCY, MERCY, MERCY

The Stilt, they called him. The Big Dipper.
Chamberlain was the man for whom
they changed the rules, because one night
he scored 100 points in a game.
And Wilt owned Pep's Musical Bar,
Broad and South, Philadelphia,
1965, where the kick-ass
Adderley sextet of the time—
Cannonball on alto, his brother
Nat on cornet, Joe Zawinul
on keyboard, Yusef Lateef on tenor,
Sam Jones, bass, and Louis Hayes, drums—
was flat-down cooking and turning out

the whole damned place. It was standing room only,
and there I was standing, in a jam-packed aisle
between bar and booths, in love with sound.
How precisely I can remember
that Yusef had launched into *Gemini*
when I felt the tap on my shoulder and turned
and looked straight into the middle button
of a splash-weave jacket and heard the voice
from way on high: *Pardon me, white man.*
What else on earth would I dream of doing?
I felt in fact it was *I* who needed
pardon, and not because I felt fear,
as I might have, the man being more than tall,

the man being wide as a truck as well,
which you couldn't tell on television—

no, not fear, but rather the total
incapacity, my own
or anyone else's, to take that night
and the muted light and the mellow feeling
from liquor, and blow every ounce of it all
into the air in one huge breath,
a breath that would somehow change the world
that I knew surrounded everybody.
Dr. King was trying to change it:
you could watch every day on t.v.
The frothing dogs and redneck cops.

The clubs. The hoses. The cattle prods.
I was just 21 in '65,
so this was likely my own first inkling
that goodwill and hope may count for nothing
and magical thinking can't even buy you
a beer if you can make your way
—*pardon me pardon me pardon me pardon me*—
past that wall of black bodies and up to the bar
and make yourself heard over harmonies
and tumbles down into dissonance
and back again of the reeds and cornet,
above the percussion, above the funky
wrenching chords that Joe broke into

next on *Mercy, Mercy, Mercy.*

MANURE: AN ADDRESS ON OLDER AGE

—for M.K. Lea (1944-1981)

That bird and thousands like it have fashioned their ratty nests
on the Four Brothers islands of Lake Champlain, where my brothers and I
would pitch a tent as boys, and by firelight sit back against
the schist and watch the summer constellations march
across the lake toward dawn. We heard whippoorwills back then
on each distant shore. We cooked simple hot dogs that tasted of heaven.

I refer to the glossy black cormorant there on that whited wharfpost,
propped on his stiffened tail, neck and head held upright
like a stalk or stick. To see that he's just this marvelous *machine*
for fishing is to see he's elegant actually, beautiful maybe.
He reclines on those feathers because his feet are so far astern
he's unbalanced on land; but they make him into an ideal swimmer.

There stands no tree, no shrub, no greenery at all on the Brothers,
the birds' manure so hot that every last thing but the cormorants
has died out there. Waste nourishes nothing. Old Hemingway
at his worst would write, *Long time ago good. Now no good.*
So check your no-good eyes from getting all wet with feeling
for a pigeon-toed John Deere tractor nodding and rusting on the margin

of that field behind us, on what poets perhaps once called a greensward.
It dozes like some benign despot, deposed, the machine. In its way
it's become a part of the system we carelessly call Nature,
its fluids long bled into ground it had tilled, a sort of deadly
manure too. Still the tractor is elegant, beautiful also,
and prompts one's vague longing for innocent Eden. Did it exist?

We know very well it didn't: in fact my brothers and I
did more than toast meats and make bonfires and stargaze; we fought like jays
over how and where to pitch the cumbersome canvas tent,
over who'd get to paddle stern, and we drank till we puked. To say so
means to recall, imagination now on a strange sort of roll,
how Hurricane Hugo came to Charleston, where I and my wife

repaired for romantic escape shortly after. There we beheld
a flock of black-crowned night herons, blown from saltmarsh to city.
They crowded a certain park's live oaks and shat all over
the flagstones on which local artists had always stood their easels
to paint, perhaps, the wondrous birds of the southern saltmarsh.
The lovely herons transformed the street life into pure hell.

Which in turn makes me think of the clutch of Canada geese that hatched
on our pond and surprised us, because after all they're so famously noisy,
and here they just showed up half-grown, no honk or murmur
all spring, and you may know how handsome these creatures appear,
and how little that comeliness counts when they crap all over your shore.
I regret to inform you I took down the shotgun. I did so, however,

only to fire above their heads till at last they left,
though I know in my heart I'd have made my aim at them more lethal
if they hadn't flown off. I want the islands back, the Brothers!
How right it would be for that slumbering tractor to burst into loudness!
How fine it seemed when geese, those exquisite flight-machines,
were only tuneful specks, passing so high, so clean.

Yellow House

You had to know the combination.
That's how you put it: how to tweak
air volume controls on the antique pump,
and from which roof valley you needed to chop
the ice dams first, and how to get
a stone-dead boiler to kick in again.

Where to aim your propane torch
at that same damned pipe just under the sink
in the kitchen that froze to death whenever
it was twenty below, not to speak of lower.
You couldn't get things too hot too fast.
If you did, the whole cold mess would burst

at the usual elbow, and you'd have to sweat
another new joint, and the water that jetted
before you could turn the valve would have turned
to instant crackling ice on the floor.
That old fake-brick linoleum floor,
no cellar below it. You were in for it now,

but good for it too because you were young
and welcomed a challenge—no children yet
to worry about, as you did about
the Round Oak stove, all filigree
and fluted finial but its firebox only
thin sheet metal that would glow so red

you sat up to watch it, afraid for the house,
for your wife upstairs. One time there lay
just moisture enough in the sand you shoveled
to damp the blaze that the stove blew the mica
right out of its door, coals scorching the boards.
Still you survived, if the marriage didn't.

Isn't it good to be out of that wreck,
that old yellow house with its corncob and paper
for insulation, its biting boreal
gales through every socket and nailhole?
And you married again. After 25 years,
it looks as though this thing has stuck.

After this quarter century,
you're in it for good now. How strange, therefore,
that you can almost think well of those days
when most of a winter meant such an adventure.
It's better now, and your walk this morning
in the deep-blue glory of February,

planet-bright snow on every branch,
and your coming home to affection and warmth—
you couldn't beat either with a stick or stone,
as your long-dead grandmother used to say
back in a time when the drifts got deeper,
the air got colder, your children were only

dreams of a future, who are grown and gone.

II. Neighbors

RECESSION

A grotesquerie for so long we all ignored it:
The mammoth plastic Santa lighting up
On the Quik-Stop's roof, presiding over pumps
That gleamed and gushed in the tarmac lot below it.

Out back, with pumps of their own, the muttering diesels.
And we, for the most part ordinary folks,
Took all for granted: the idling semis' smoke,
The fuel that streamed into our tanks, above all

Our livelihoods. We stepped indoors to talk
With friends, shared coffee, read the local paper,
Heavy with news of hard times now. We shiver.
Our afternoons are gone. At five o'clock

—Once we gave the matter little thought—
Our Santa Claus no longer flares with light.

Garnett and Leon in December

Garnett's wrinkles
would hold a week

of rain. His knuckles
are small white onions.

Each yarn of each
sounds like *farewell*

here in December.
Afternoon like night

when Garnett feeds chickens,
he hears more than sees them.

Leon clenches
his pipe and puffs

with a maul to his woodpile
at the bottom of which

I long to imagine
a dark iron spike

in a log which the fabled
river-drivers

followed downstream
till it ended here.

Stars grow sharp
to announce the cold.

The cold. Put that
in your pipe and smoke it.

Leon inhales
and studies the wood.

Garnett's face
could hold the flood.

Dandelion Pickers

Under the garish fast-food billboard,
        which insults a field on Route 10,
always in tilth before the farm
        like so many others went down
and its owners dispersed—under that come-on
        for the famous Happy Meal,
two men of indeterminate age

        are plucking dandelions
before they bud. By the ditch, their crippled
        Ford, a part of the scene.
Which is elemental. Or so I conclude.
        Where must they live? In the car?
Out of old habit, I'm searching my mind,
        rifling that old attic

to put things in their place. The Ford
        seems to hold what little they have:
it's piled to the panels, and even the transom
        in back is stacked with what look
like documents of some kind, their contents
        shakily scanned by the bobblehead
hula girl at her central post

        among them, the pale sheets heaped
at her flanks like stale snow. There are puddles along
        the shoulder, smudges of gray
under the day's own gray, the gatherers'
        faces darker than they are,
all tarnish and whisker, booze-blossom and grime.
        I sigh. And scold myself,

having no notion at all what's what
          with these two men at their labor.
Shut up, I think, *You have no idea.*
          I ought just to keep on moving.
The greens can be used as well to make
          a wine that could hammer you
right out of your lousy nosy skull.

          Though I'm probably driving too fast,
I can make out, behind the pair
          and over the granite knoll,
two turkey vultures, birds reputed
          to vomit on interlopers.
And yet they look graceful—a sign of spring,
          no matter the drizzle, the cold.

What little they have. The phrase keeps ringing,
          and yet the men may have something:
my final glimpse as I hurtle by
          is of slick sacks bulged
by the acid edible dandelion leaves.
          I know they're only weeds,
although it's never seemed to me easy

          to distinguish them from flowers.
I hate how my mind keeps looking for wordplay,
          figure, metaphor:
The birds, the knoll, the junker Ford,
          the dirty men on their knees,
and above all that grayer-than-gray of the day . . . .
          In the old kids' pastime, you blew

on the fluff of fullblown dandelions
      and watched it float away
to wherever the slightest breeze might take it.
      It used to make me feel
a bit like a god, I think. Or did it?
      I'm working to liken the pickers
to fluff I can scatter abroad on the winds.

      Shut up, I breathe, *and drive.*
What's wrong with me? What manner of man
      would long to go back and read
among that old car's tattered pages?
      What if the men feel proud?
What if they chose a life and, choosing,
      concluded it was good?

Six Lies about Nature, Ending with a Soul-Tune Line

—*remembering Louis Cattani*

That it is economical—
>One year those scarlet tanagers came blown untimely
>North from Carolina on a great storm's gale all reckless
>To be sown on this cold landscape amid old snow gone grimy
>And were thus bright ruined flowershapes in their thousands.
>>Thousands.

Or a harmony—
>I could see from the outcrop of runneled granite above that clearing
>The bitch coyote begin to eat the hare who screamed
>Like a woman or child and went on living while it was dying
>As ravens who'd coasted to treetops sat out their wait. And
>>preened.

Or "never did betray the heart that loved her"—
>They thought at first that Lou had pulled a muscle in his neck
>While he was out on the water paddling and drawing good breath
>>and loving
>Autumn's harlequin hues along the banks and ducks
>That splashed among ripe acorns falling in. And floating.

Or is somehow pure, non-human—
>Rapine and profligacy are parts of it too and Lou's tumor
>And despots and grim lust for lucre and any berserker contraption
>That keeps on paving incalculable animation under
>Or even a couple grown savage together. Their one last attraction.

Or restores—
>Since a person may lose a wife or child or father or mother
>And Time which is nature as well will be a poor healer no matter

That we sit on a saltwhite beach or under some favorite star
For our wounds still feel ragged as if we were being eaten. We are.

Or can solace entirely—
    That it will in the words of the great Wilson Pickett from years
        gone by
    One of these early mornings be wiping my weeping eye.

Dubber's Cur

—for John Engels (1931 – 2007)

At last one day I used a trick you may have heard of:
I loaded a 12-gauge shell
with rocksalt and shot him from distance enough I'd hurt him plenty
but do no actual harm.
He gave a satisfactory yelp and bolted over
our ridge, blond blur of sinew.

A scary thing to look at, he must be partly pit bull
—the telltale eyes and boxy
countenance—but mixed with something much, much bigger.
He's a brute, all maw and chest.
And yet as far as I can tell there's no mean streak
in Buddy, who's not to blame:

Dubber just can't seem to keep him home. Or won't.
Every morning Buddy
winds our own dogs up, and pees on each last post
and door and flowerstalk.
That day of the shooting, I told myself I'd had enough
this time, and told my family,

"We won't see *him* again." In only a matter of hours
he climbed back up to us
from that junkheap ramble of trailers, pickups, scrap iron, tires,
down where Dubber lives
with his wife by common law and two young roly daughters
still at home, each girl

with at least one child of her own. The Lord knows how they keep
body and soul together.
Some time later—and who can say how a thing can start
to brew in a person's mind?—
while driving back from the upscale market five towns south,
hauling salmon, French bread,

organic greens in our foreign car, I came to think
how likely it was that Buddy
had wandered in once more to lift his leg somewhere.
All our house dogs, meanwhile,
who in fact should daily bark their thanks to God they *are*
just that, house dogs, inside,

not mixing it up with him—our dogs would again be slavering
on the windows, howling at Buddy.
I swore by habit, then somehow felt: *At times your life
can lift you from the factual.*
I was more than glad for that, no matter it came so sudden,
and didn't make any sense,

and doesn't accord with anything a man could prove
or defend, or even want to.
In that same moment, I envisioned my penniless neighbor's mongrel,
his dauntless, tireless Buddy,
trotting his usual beat up the face of that murderous ridge
leaving his wretched gang

to eke out its day, the sun pouring down through a crack in the mountains
buttery in the vision
on the dog's thick fur, heraldic. And he seemed an admirable creature,
if only for his patience.
More: the house and hovels, the twisted wrecks of chassis
and antique farm machines

all seemed to assume a kindred glow, and so seemed part
of something much, much bigger.
The wetnose kids, the scrabbling barncats, pullets, poults,
the scrawny pony and weedy
garden plot . . . . Forgive me,

but these all testified to a light in each of us,
though don't embarrass me,
don't ask a thing about it. Instead, let me ask *you*:
have you not in your wandering
a world that you've done your own small part like me to soil,
not sometimes felt a purpose?

Some might shoot you for it, granted. It remains
a purpose, though, and though
I almost see you lift the gun, you may have sensed
a near-exalting rightness
in doggedly keeping at it, just as Dubber's cur
keeps at his climb, shows up.

EARLY LIFE

All the pastor's years of serving his Lord
and humankind seem nothing now.
His congregation has long resigned itself
to anecdotal, meandering sermons.
But how forgive his mixing the liturgy
of welcome to a new church member
with the ceremony—however it may be related—
of baptism? The poor young parents

blush and fidget while veteran members feel
something between impatience and rage.
The minister and infant, robed and sleeping,
appear serene, above it all,
the one too young, even awake, to know
what goes on here and the other unable
to keep intact his thinking. Painful pauses.
Autumn rain on the roof like gunfire.

Of course there are some members who, approaching
the old man's age, feel sympathy
as he stands bemused and calm, his wan blue eyes
entirely empty, like the font he forgot
to fill before the service got underway.
No one knows that yet. He's always
been a reflective sort of man, concerned
with important matters. No one knows

what to do with him. Arriving late this morning
yet again, he plucked a flower
from the vestry garden, and wears it jauntily

in a hole in his cassock. You might compare
his look to some young man's of a certain era
setting out on a certain evening
to visit with a woman, a girl really,
the one he wants to be his wife.

As the poet said, The world lies all before them.
Early life. When a deacon whispers
into his ear, the pastor cocks his head
and finds a momentary return
to the requisite rite. Of course the empty font
remains a problem. The girl he wed
in fact is decades dead. The pastor seems
to shun the mention of her name,

though seasoned congregants admired and liked her.
No one knows or probes his motives,
even if there are members who, approaching
the old man's age, still mourn and miss her.
Forget the font. Let's leave him with his aster
still in place, and memories
of other time now fusing with whatever
he may be musing as he lifts the child,

who, just awakened, grasps the flower
and babbles so brightly the pastor smiles.

Stump's Hernia

We wince to think of laying hands on that node
and wouldn't, God in heaven, wouldn't.
Not for thousands of dollars, not at knifepoint.
And we shudder, uncertain what kind of catastrophe impends
when it bursts and spews its pent-in contents.

We all agree: *That thing must be a time bomb.*
Cantaloupe-sized, it pokes a rough nose
from between Stump's low-riding belt and high-riding T-shirt,
whose bib is all juices and oils and unutterables that attend
Stump's weekend calling: hauler of refuse,

hefter of bag after reeking bag of things
we all want gone. On every Sunday,
in every weather, he wears that flimsy shirt
above the gloss-green trousers and under the sort of hat
that people used to call a porkpie.

We can't help noticing, though, that he's always smiling,
greeting us through our kitchen windows
while we guiltily linger at breakfast, or over the paper.
Why won't he get it fixed? Each of us hopes the explosion
will happen elsewhere. Stump's hail-fellow-

well-met astounds us meanwhile. Perhaps he's depressed,
and somehow figures no good can come
of changing what's what. We need an explanation.
We need to account for the man without some rhapsody
on the Happy Poor, which we know would be wrong.

Still, we hate being mired like this in confusion,
making no sense of how in May,
as the blackflies strafe his face, for instance, he never
raises a hand for a swat, and how he flaunts that knob,
which catches the light of a newborn day.

Stump flies Old Glory from his beat-up truck's antenna,
but the radio's dead, so his only choices
are corny country songs from an antique tape deck.
On the seat, a bag of Fritos shudders with the quiver of diesel,
with the whining steel guitars and voices.

"Jesus May Love You, But I Don't" is one of his favorites.
And sometimes it seems, when we see Stump grin,
his hernia swinging brightly, as if he danced:
sometimes, we'd swear, the stench and music and birdsong and clouds
and even the chip-sack—all thrum as one.

Rodney Fallen

I'd cut a bit less than I thought last spring for the shed,
and so late winter I called up Rodney Sweet.
There was never a man better named. He's touched in the head,
some say, a Bible-thumper. That's fine by me,

since he does all right in the world with his two big rules:
Love God and your neighbor. That means his wood is good—
full cords, no popple or piss-elm. I'd been a fool,
and so felt more than lucky that Rodney still had

something on hand, and the whole of it fine rock maple.
He won't often sell by the half, but a half-cord would do,
I told him. Rodney has often called me *faithful*,
and he claims to like my trade for that, although

truth is I'm only a doubtful, unsteady client.
Maybe it's just that we see some things eye-to-eye.
Speaking of eyes, his own are blue as heaven.
You notice that right off, and so when the ice

sent him arcing that noon, his feet straight up in the air,
and he crashed to hard ground and all but knocked out his brains
and lay gut-up like a drunk in some shitface bar,
the kind of place in which he'd never be seen,

and those eyes showed flat and sightless, it seemed the world
went down along with him, and I got worried,
to say it mildly. I kept calling, "Rodney? Rodney?"—
like a life's most urgent question—and against my will

I imagined nothing at all in that skyward gaze,
and then I looked skyward also, to where the awful
crows were fighting the blow, the senseless trees
turning dark on the hills under sleetclouds that shuffled and mumbled

with only the jittery flags of beech and oak,
pallid and brown, making minimal gesture
against the shadows' grizzle. There on the snow,
his blood looked dimmer still, and all the other

colors leached off and I stood stupefied
as I contemplated Rodney. Rodney fallen.
Then the blue eyes blinked, he looked at me and smiled,
and spoke at last: "The Man up there's been trying

to pound some sense in this head for a long, long time."
O Jesus, I swear the first spring sun broke through
and the thaw began, and wrens and warblers would come.
Rodney stood, and there'd be vireos

and wrens and moon and mice and love and deer
and courage, kestrels, warmth, another year.

III. Birds, a Farrago

Birds, a Farrago

I. (Black terns)

Slight soreness, almost trifling:
it began in both thumbs, symmetric. Still
he could scratch his head at the start with either hand
and speculate, Now what's all *this?*
He couldn't look ahead.
Had he been able,
he'd not have imagined himself unable
to rise from his chair without someone to help him.

That was the summer
of his sixtieth year, of the rare black terns,
rare summer.
He'd often come on a graceful pair
near Lotts Cove Point,
at what he thought must surely be
the southmost edge of their range.
Sometimes they flew close enough for him
to distinguish the smart sable spots
behind each eye. Non-breeding plumage.

He could still ply the paddle for hours, and did.
Just to see what he could see.
The twinge in his hands must owe itself to that:
his paddle dipping, making its J,
arcing and dropping,
lifted, pulled.

The second week of August: all downlake blow.
It was hard to hold the slight boat upright.
The terns would gather
a yard from the wind then give back two
till at last they relented,
wheeling home to Briar Bog.
A man, he thought, should delight in merest
comings and goings, like the birds'.
Washed by the glory of a clear morning sun,
the eyeblink glint off a slim wing seemed
a wonder. A wonder a day:
he reckoned that much should hold him.
Come September it was feet, wrists, knees.
If miracles indeed were rife
in the daily world,
by then he craved just the one.

II. (Milady)

Dear Lady Doctor called it
post-viral arthropathy.
Mouth-filling locution, after which she went terse:
It will, she said, *be gone.*

But for two rheumatologists
at two high-end clinics,
the adjective was *rheumatoid.*
Milady's response? *Well, I'm not buying.*
Those paddle trips past bouldery shores
came often to mind as autumn winged toward

winter:
passages through a distant Eden
denied to him forever.

The terns now prompted pique,
the ease with which they hovered and danced
a thing to revile. So just as well,
his unfitness to grip a gun.
He might have shot them.
But such unpardonable thought was idle
in any case, the summer gone,
the terns long gone
—not to return and he knew it.

Still he pictured his inexcusable murder,
the lead bird crumpling up like a teal
fired upon from a blind,
falling with a small sad splash to the surface
and then the other.
Two tiny ripples on the flatted lake,
then nothing.

Nothing at least for a man
to see from a distance.

III. (Crow and vulture)

He should never have driven the roads in those days,
neck-locked, unable to swivel
his head, to check both ways for traffic.

Nor could he ply his longtime habit
of scanning the sky for things in flight,
though now and then the sky
came down to him

in the shapes of crow and vulture,
which hopped off the shoulder from this or that
vile carcass as stiffly he motored by.

Once two redneck boys, enraged,
hung tight to his bumper for miles
after he'd cut them off unknowing.
When at last they passed him they left off screaming.
He could feel his body throb and feel
the pursuers' judgment,
as if he'd heard it right out loud—
sad old man.

October leafage sharp as pain on the sidehills.

He prayed Dear Lady Doctor was right.
It seemed as if in fact it was she
to whom he kept praying,
because in wilder moments his brain would image
himself as a kind of roadkill,
the searing, stabbing thrills in his joints
not picked away with the rest, however.

Specialists, the other doctors,
they must know more than milady.

Things seemed dauntingly stacked against
a sad old man.

IV. (*Pale moth aloft*)

All the physicians urged him to keep on moving
as much as he could. He did so
clear through November as much as he could,
and of such effort made small song:

A white moth dances in place
        over ledge just north of our house,
though the snow comes hard.
        What keeps such a fluttering thing

from being instantly crushed?
        Old folks around here call
these white moths souls
        that have gone abroad for a walk,

a glide, a gander, a sail,
        whatever. To be a soul:
I'd like to be only
        a soul, because lately flesh

seems all I ever can be
        —brute fleshly yen to be healthy.
The doctor urges me
        to move my bones if I'm able.

And so I do, though my gait
       is at very best an amble.
The mothflight's slower—
       a hover, stationary.

However then can it keep
       abreast of me? It is
a spirit. Maybe.
       I ache to believe, to believe

in something once again.
       The moth's wings aren't really white
but like beech leaves that cling
       through winter. Like winter tonight,

the cold arriving early, cold
       seeming as though it may stay.
The wings are ecru,
       I think, always the aesthete at play.

Or perhaps they're beige or dun.
       As if such a matter mattered.
Something must matter.
       I do have daughters and sons—

and a granddaughter now. I would leave them
       some sense of the world beside
dumb resignation:
       I, who had thought distinctions

were part of a valuable life.
        Perhaps they're part of the problem.
Despair/Desire.
        I'm inept enough as a teacher,

yet I long to leave the children
        more than fairy tale
or folk surmise,
        more than some pale moth hung

beside the drearying woods
        of November, under these skies
that sag with snow.
        Is there anything more, I wonder,

than my own appetitive will
        in imagining that I see
some sign in what floats
        before me? How distinguish

my yearning from faith? Can the dance
        of this bug or spirit against
hard ledge that whitens
        darkly and darkening mulch,

make a parable transcending
        either/or, a freeing
I can almost feel
        within my very being?

V. (*Black like ravens*)

That was exactly and only song,
lyrical, pitiable, highflown
self-directed blather . . .
though he did rather like that figure
of the floating moth.

And yet black tern, pale moth—what matter?

Each betokened truth:
what flew reminded him what he didn't do
and what he couldn't.

And the others in his life,
friends and children, his wife,
the baby girlchild?

No matter either.
It would be months before he knew
he'd been flying more and more deeply all that while
into the raven-black cave of self.

VI. (*Not even a jay*)

With his throbbing fingers he'd twisted sprigs off a fir to fill
his study with sweet mild scent. The frequent thought of his oldest child's
first child, the nails of her fingers so tiny
and nacred, had frequently made his breath go shallow.
Why then amid such blessedness—

he'd never had to hunger, nor lust for things,
having all he could need, a wondrous wife,
a cherished landscape, and all their children better
than he'd ever been, and stronger:
why then should he look away today
from all of that and find the world as he had known it
become a mist?

Where was the sun,
which had danced just moments ago
on the stony ridge above the meadow
and guarded the meadow?
It had sunk into shadow before the day
should demand that sun be down,
be dead and gone:

no birds in the heavens, not even
the ravenous jays
ubiquitous in any normal December.

Near-blinded by this silent ambush of evening
he considered the way he'd lived
and hoped to keep on living
as husband, father, citizen, neighbor:
it was merest vapor,
himself a vapor.

Even ego might vanish,
existence a palimpsest of emptiness,
the sun's disappearance boding anullment

of his lesser light.
He doused the desktop lamp.
What in his blindness did the wrecked Earl say?
I see it feelingly.
Just so he meant to rise and feel for his chair
and push it back and feel for his door
and pass into a house he pictured as gone
all ghostly, scarce-discernible too—blank window-
panes, piano, photos in frames—
and to feel for his loved ones
and to join them, the specters, at family supper.

Someone would have to come
and pull him up however.

VII. (*Rara avis*)

Not like other terns.
Sometimes hiking inland he'd seen them, hawking
insects in conifer woods.
Their population was ebbing, all sources informed him.
Much later he'd reprimand himself:
imagine—a fantasy
of gunning down this *rara avis!*

His rage, he knew, was ebbing too.
He rather missed it.
Or rather he chafed at having lost it

in its earlier form, original vigor,
such loss implying that time was moving
his mind toward meek acceptance.

He did not try to hike anymore,
nor even to walk,
no matter Lady Doctor's instructions.

VIII. (Brown kite, blood horse)

He had daydreams as he sat unmoving there. One of them featured
white Lipizzaners
that he'd seen in Europe once. He'd once imagined *himself*
a performing stallion. Then years flew by and his joints caught fire.
He could remember

how he writhed, impatient, in the hotel bed, avid to walk
in morning air,
superbly able-bodied, through the hard-edged early shadows
striate on bright June fields. But he shied and winced at a scream
from one of the mares,

a stud roaring back—at the fear and menace that melded in sound.
A stream clear as ether
glistened to westward. He took for it. Two honeymooners
smiled and hailed him, *Grüss Gott!* They made a more than handsome
couple, either

astride a dark dappled colt of some wraith-pale dam and sire.
He didn't then dream
his good fortune in having seen so much. How could he have missed it?
He remembered, above the trill of the brook, the hollow clop
of a carriage team,

how he'd thought he might enjoy such a tour—a thought to be quelled.
He'd walk *bei Gott!*
The boulders sprawled to either side, all wraithlike too
in a hazel thicket. A fox's track made a single line
in the marl and mud.

He followed a fence of lichened rock through shivering woods
and dazzled dells.
It spiralled like thoughts of a man like him, alone on a visit.
All of this, for whatever reason, felt strange and familiar
at once. Deep holes

showed where the limestone cap had failed in so many places.
A spiralling kite
above was looking down for rodents in new-mown fields.
He couldn't resist trite fantasies of soaring so.
When his malady hit

in afteryears, his fantasy was of common earth
beneath his feet.
Full of all this recall, the daydream tugged like a horse
at its tether. Soon that Austrian pair, having cantered their mounts
to a spume of sweat,

swung down to ground and went back hand in hand to their rented room.
He'd seen such things,
he'd known such things. Beyond the woodlot he came on a paddock
where a stallion farted and jogged, all lordly animus.
In a trainer's hand,

one end of a longe-line, which the bloodhorse accepted, as he didn't have to,
all muscle and sheen,
each of his lusty gaits a dance. Bright shale on the mountains,
bright clouds and sky—all centered now on the pivoting stud,
unburdened gleam

of sun on his testes. As for himself, he was only a tourist
who suddenly ached
for home. And here he was at home, all stab and ache,
far off from such a fresh and brilliant spring. In mind
the fierce kite stooped.

IX. (*Each sparrow that falls . . .*)

> *As high as we have mounted in delight*
> *In our dejection do we sink as low.*

Once, out camping alone, he thought of that Nature Poet.
Yet he wouldn't have claimed it was dejection
he felt. Not delight either.
He had gulped his rough food down, and now he played
at comprehending a life of privation,
his satiety spawning a counter-vision
of a filthy shivering homeless figure,
       calling out to passersby for compassion,

Have a heart. But no one dropped one coin in his cup.
Wind in the alley hailed cinders against him.
This sort of derelict made
an outdoorsman perforce in the gun-blue night: *homeless*
seemed feeble abstraction. It felt easy to hate him
somehow—unless like the Nature Poet one could imagine
a *mystical* home, great Oneness.
       As the camper couldn't. A shock of memory blocked him.

He closed his eyes against the woodsmoke and entered a scene
of his own rapacity years back:
Precisely as if at home,
a perching sparrow called to other sparrows
on the ground among plump chickens that scratched
and eyed the smaller birds as they scrabbled for grub and grit,
the pests! The hens would have liked to kill them,
       and he for some reason was on their side. He shot

the dispensable sparrow down from its willow. Oh nothing was hallowed
to the boy, that muddle of motiveless needs.
He dug under feather and flesh
for the sparrow's heart, a steaming purple pip
forever reduced to stillness. How weak
his .22 had sounded in the March gale's shriek.
The weakness enraged him. He knew
       little of what he was doing, but any brute act

could satisfy him: he pinched the steaming heart in his hand.
Murders revealed his obscure compulsions:
why else that innocent songbird,
those gasping sunfish in buckets, those pink nestling mice?
The camper's fire grew cool in that late late season.
Would he ever know redemption? All the old poems had failed him.
Could someone like him grow generous?
      The fallen sparrow lived on, implacable witness.

X. (Loons and chemicals)

Milady's New Year's gift:
a medication called Prednisone.
Now he could rise and walk and act as if
this horror were not
to stay with him forever.
Relief untold, untellable.

The wind was coming north that day.
the lake of the terns sealed over,
with any boat left in it
locked fast for all the rest of winter.

Why then the thought of a hen loon,
chick on her back,
of her call—not the the mournful wail
but the "crazy," laughing cackle?
At summer's end the chick would be able too
to take to air, but would need the lift
of a wind like this: He felt it
course downlake, the birds shearing waves till at last

the broad wings worked their wonder
and the two loons turned in a trice to specks
and then were gone.

That August the terns had ridden and fought the gale.

He might shy from the very notion of forever
swallowing some steroid pill,
afraid for his body's system—but how
had he ever in any case named
that system *immune?*

And *forever:* to a man of his age the concept
felt far much less than endless.
Moreover he'd been so sore so long
and would keep on being sore
without the daily dose of small bitter tablets,
one on rising and one at evening,
that no matter his night thoughts: just being
alive again like this seemed superabundance.

He watched the other old concept—
miracle—fly up and shine.

XI. (Golden-crowned kinglets)

He awakened on February first, stunned again by that odd
old wonder: how quickly *old* had come. Of course if his will had been done
he'd have risen youthful, but age was here, he'd own it, and he thanked his god

for the absence today of companion pain, no matter he owed that to pills.
As he had since he was younger, he put on snowshoes and clambered over
drifts and up a daunting granite bluff. As much by will

as muscle he powered on through powder for the view from there. A blessing:
eastward the white White Mountains all seemed to be staring placidly down on
ice-dams hunched in the river. He kicked his feet out of leather bindings

to climb a tree. West, a neighbor's strange herd of alpacas milled,
full-wooled, though mere months back—short-shorn, with feeble reeds for necks
—they were fragile creatures, naked, susceptible, silly. Same as us all.

Through his teeth he forced out air—birdwatcher trick—and imagined a lisping
cloud, his sounds small jets of steam. Cloud full of birds, he dreamed.
Did an eagle shriek? Too far to tell. But kinglets were suddenly flying

from his south to land all around, on his limb and all the way up to the crown,
then were gone so quickly he all but missed the marvel: the kinglets come.

XII. *(Scavengers, grackles)*

The day's soft glow made a later climb worth the effort.
A raven, old familiar, scolded and swooped,

protecting the nest she'd kept for years in that spruce.
But he was harmless, he was looking *down* where the river

sluiced past its banks, which were slow to green as ever.
Two yearling deer stood out on flooded ground

soon to be broken: in turn, when fall had come,
shivering cornrows would wait out there for the thresher.

Yes, he'd looked up when he got there, had lain on the earth,
face skyward, as if his life had *future* in it.

As now it did, he believed, though vultures didn't.
How determined, devoted the wild things were in their search,

having only one motive: sustenance, and soon.
Three birds glided low; he could see their eyes.

He, who'd been dreaming how wide the wide world was,
even this portion he climbed on and claimed for his own.

He stood to scare off the vultures and scare off the thoughts
such birds can bring, both disconcerting and banal.

He kept watching the timid deer: they fed and startled,
trotted a few quick yards before they paused

to look over their shoulders. *They can't know where I am,
nor who*, he thought, in this all-subsuming shine:

the river misting, the mist gone silver in sun,
the yearlings' hides as well, and the metal domes

of silos, the commonwealth of blackbirds that gleamed
from that heartbreak riverside hedge of tall dead elms.

XIII. (*Juncos*)

He'd always loved them,
small slate smudges
at the feeder again, small signs again
of lingering winter, one could say,
but in their northering signals
of spring aborning too.

Dear Lady Doctor said *Go off those pills*,
he did, and reverted to wholeness.

It was simple as that, too simple perhaps,
as if what had seemed
a nasty tale turned out benign unduly
soon, devoid of explanation

that he or anyone possessed
of reason might find some tenable way to accept.

He didn't know, he'd never know what took him.
Nobody would.

He was spared, was all—*hosanna,*
vernal equinox—
great god in heaven.

XIV. (*Spring flocks*)

Why had it always been birds with him,
the summer tern,
flash-capped kinglet in winter,
that sparrow he slaughtered, unthinking, young?

Birds were future and memory both,
rebuke and consolation.
Might that be it?

He let his beloved humans back
into his world, flew out of solitude
of self, remembered all that had ever mattered,
full of love and gratitude, not least
for Dear Lady Doctor, prophet,
priestess, healer,

and once again in his life looked forward
among so many other things

to the way that flying things
would be arriving soon enough in their order.
No, not *order*: a farrago, hallowed—
Vesper Sparrow
Chipping Sparrow
Tree Swallow
Barn Swallow

He missed the *Whippoorwill,*
which nevermore chanted in the region's fields.

House Wren
Ovenbird
Wood Thrush
Ruby-throated Hummingbird
Goldfinch
Yellow Warbler
Wood Pewee
Kingbird

The spring would come, whatever might befall him,
and to know as much
was to dream for some reason the sound of diving nighthawks,
the *boom* of their wings in their plunges
a wonder, tiny but more than tiny after
all he'd known and felt and seen.

And the terns, the terns in mating plumage:
in their way he knew they'd be there forever,
blackish but beyond all depiction clean.

IV. Dispute with Thomas Hardy

DIVINATION

Under the hornbeam you always lean on in summer for ease from whatever hike
the day has chosen for you, there's a sun-paled wishbone, small almost to infinite.

Birdbone.

Warbler? Creeper? Wren? No matter, except that the bone may move a mind,
if, that is, it wants to be moved, wants for instance to identify

the killer.

Predator? Sickness? Weather? And yet such questions are no matter either. Somewhere
you've read of a tribe or nation—which tribe, which nation appears likewise to be

unimportant—

who used the sterna of birds for divination. So you pinch the pin-thin arms
of the bone and aim it outward over a valley so vast just now there can be

no way

to read it, but what on earth would that signify, *to read it?* You gave away
any claim to science so many years back that now the sortings of schist from granite

in the vista,

of conifer from hardwood timber, of this cloud from that, will serve no purpose.
And what could ever be meant by *purpose?* For you there's nothing higher encoded

in Nature.

Still you wear the human wound: your urge for significance throbs like a bruise.
And for whatever reason the bone, the physical bright-white bone itself, appears

miraculous,

even though you know it's nothing against the continents and seas, afire
with murder and rapine. *Put down the wishbone*, you say to yourself. *Lie back against*

your hornbeam.

You know you forge your construals from urgent dreams. Yet you persist: you lean
forward, tense, gripping those near-invisible calcified tines in front

of your heart,

and in the bone's knuckle you feel a shiver—you *do!*—then a microscopic bucking,
as if you reined a horse so tiny that its only capacity was a stirring

of air,

its own mere speck of it. You choose to think something's out there. You name it hope.
You choose that name. And whatever superstition prompts the conviction, you're sure

—you insist

on being sure—it's there, beneath the selfsame hornbeam which you're pleased to lean on in summer, in whatever ramble occurs to you on whatever day,

for ease.

The Walker

—for Robin

I see him out here yet again and am right off desperate to tell you
about him again because— If he can walk these merciless miles
in a day forever and ever as you know he does
in all weathers since the coronary and bypass

from his out-of-plumb lone hovel up there on German Ridge
all the way south on Route 5 past where the mean geese live
that hiss and charge at him though he pays no attention whatever
to their fierceness and possessiveness but tramps along on and on

and at length turns back toward home I assume where no one lives but him
because I've passed him coming and going— If I can notice him
for instance in winter when the logging trailers slosh him
as they stampede by and he never misses a beat nor raises an eye

nor pauses in dogday summer when most of us are dreaming of coolness
by the pond near Hattie's Knoll that he marches dogged oblivious past
and in spring when he seems not to respond in the least to the peepers'
melodies or the warblers' nor in mid-autumn to the frantic maples

and poplars and ashes that spread their madness on the far White
    Mountains
already snow-dusted across the wind-lathered river
though oh how you and I have adored that foam and fire—
If he can so persist in walking mile upon mile upon mile upon mile

day upon day upon day upon day to preserve his heart and if I
can go on driving past him like this as he makes his slow slow progress
though progress seems an odd word for something that gets nowhere
and never appears to end and is really in fact all he does anymore—

If he can keep at it forever and I can keep looking on at him
then it means that my heart's mad hopeless dream many miles and miles
and years down the road will after all have turned out true
because he'll be there to be walking and I to be watching

and I'll still have you

HEIMATSLOSIGKEIT

Why on earth would I remember this or any other word
in German, which I never really learned? It was used by some brainy scholar
in a book I read in a time when I thought I wanted to be a brainy scholar.
He put a twist on the meaning. My seldom considered German dictionary
called it simply *homelessness*, but for the scholar the word meant *thrown-ness*,
exemplified by Adam and Eve's condition when they got themselves chucked out
of the garden. But why would I summon Adam or Eve or Eden on a certain
   evening,

Late March, Vermont, while hiking thick woods, unbrainily, without my
   snowshoes?
A mile or so, then I started to break through grimy crust with every step,
and today I'm left to guess why such a term—unbidden, highfalutin—
would leap to mind. My endurance running low, it may have been I feared
I'd never again see home, my legs like sashweight iron, zinc-colored sun
slithering nightward down the blackened hills. But no, of course I'd survive,
   for once
having a pack full of extra clothes on my back. It was really no more than that:

Speculation, same as now. I wasn't really in physical danger,
or not of dying unhoused in any case. And so it was perhaps
that a sort of meta-physical thrown-ness, subtle as Satan, slid itself
into a brain that I had tried to set as free as it wanted to be.
I do that whenever I walk this landscape. I've never been much for
   philosophy—
abstracted thought, as Huck Finn said of something else, *too many for me*—
so I may fit Flannery O'Connor's self-description as "a person

74

Constitutionally innocent of theory but with certain preoccupations."
Whatever my own proccupations, it's likely as not that they're much
    different
from so great an author's. Who's to say? Truth is, as we're looking here for
    truth—
or at least I am, or was, I believe, when *Heimatslosigkeit* hopped in
so strangely to my ken—I've never quite defined my preoccupations.
A lot of Nature. A lot of Love. A lot of Family. A little at least
of this and that. But as I was lying safe in my own bed last night

I started meditating on things I call important, though I can't fit them
even into the sort of polysyllabic satchel that German allows.
Yes I struggled yesterday to make my way, but at least I was headed *home*.
Whereas Evie Benson, who lives or rather lived beside the railroad tracks,
got burned out two weeks ago. I saw her standing in front of our general store
a day or so after. She held what little she'd managed to save in a plastic bag
that showed the logo of some chain drugstore, and with her Denison Carter,
    to whom

I'd never paid a lot of mind: the merest nod, a vague hello.
Evie had always been the very figure of loneliness to me.
No husband, no children. And she never belonged to the Women's Club or
    local church
or anything else I could think of, though it was seldom I thought of Evie
    either,
if truth be known. Yet I watched as Denny offered her his paper cup
of coffee and handed her his powdery doughnut, and when she blew on the cup
and dunked the doughnut and ate it, I thought a thought so embarrasingly
    bland,

So far from metaphysical, it almost threw me. But I'll speak it here:
Some people still know how to be kind. And a thought so simple brought me
  to tears.

DISPUTE WITH THOMAS HARDY

The smile on your mouth was the deadest thing
Alive enough to have strength to die.
—"Neutral Tones"

It won't last long, this snow that sheathes
       the dooryard pine in April and lays
its pale doomed cover on the slope behind.
       Crocuses, just tall enough,
are poking their small pink noses through.
       It's clear they're alive enough to live
though April's gale is artillery-loud.
       What's left of ice around the pond
in town looks rough as predators' teeth.
       Somewhere a fisher rips open a mouse.

There's much I too may try to cover,
       which is why perhaps I feel strange gladness
to watch the omni-inclusive white
       subsume the neutral tones that pushed
our brilliant poet to ponder death
       and love's deception, its cruelty.
We've been together, my love and I,
       near three decades, which have scudded by
like these sideways flakes. My mortal wife . . .
       There *can* come pangs. But freshets have started

to wander the brush and leave their signs.
       Soon we'll find the trillium,
the painted kind, in the hidden place,
       which I discovered ten springs ago
and which since then I've kept a secret
       from all but her—from even our children;
and the valley's white-faced Herefords
       dropped new calves while winter endured.

Mud and blood yet cling to the cows
        but the calves shine clean as a colorful dream.

What dream would be mine? That life go on,
        that all humanity go on.
No more than dream, of course, I know,
        the planet heating up, the cretin
politicians rattling swords,
        as if, by counter-logic, war
transmuted the earth into something saintly.
        The harder facts conspire against me.
Yet to know as much is to make me cling
        the harder to gifts apparently given

without my having at all to deserve them:
        flowers, animals, glinting trees,
and a disposition that moves me here
        to disputation with my great better,
in spite of all my darker doubt.
        Inkling of something soon to come down
like rain upon mown grass, as showers
        that water the earth. Some Lordly power,
or at least new weather. Or the smile on the mouth
        of that lover-wife, which blinds like snow.

Or the road agent waving from his bright-red plow
        as it smoothes the drifted back lanes over.

Young of the Year

— for Cora Jane Lea

A small hare's stride displays itself in snowdust up on this knob
that we call The Lookout. *Young of the year.*
I whisper the term our old folks use to name
a prior spring's wild things—or the year itself, young year.

New grandfather now, have I a right to the phrase? I speak it no matter.
To me its assonance appeals;
its heft of optimism and forward-looking
correct a mood. It's a counter-cry to my vain appeals

to some power unseen that it remake me into a youthful man,
that it change this world. I scrutinize
a certain mountain's western flank, ravines
turned to fat white rivers in winter. I likewise scrutinize

myself in relation to mountain. I used to *charge* her up and down
in a slim few hours. Today I wonder
if I'll climb there again, my strength and stamina less
than once they were. What isn't? The mountain. The mountain's a wonder.

With inner eyes I see its trees, knee-high at 4000 feet.
I see myself step onto aprons of stone
at her summit. I'd never have dreamed how much I'd love it,
loving that child. In youth the thought would have turned me to stone.

On The Lookout's granite, a wisp—unidentifiable, blooded—of fur.
So many hundreds and thousands of victims
in a cruel season. Behind the mountain an airplane
aroar to put me in mind of bombers searching out victims.

In time it may even be that I'll prefer to see her from here,
not here from her. I mean the mountain.
Wonders never cease, it's rightly said.
Those inner eyes go back and forth from infant to mountain,

where even now in January the hardwoods' fraught tight buds
display their purple, enduring signal
of spring. Which will come. Which has never failed to come.
Already the girl and I have developed private signals:

I can waggle my tongue at her, or flutter my fingers, and make her smile.
I can lie back humming in uncanny peace,
child on my chest, and I can remember how
I held her father. But I think I hold her better. Peace:

perhaps it's for this one exchanges his further dreams. And perhaps I know
what's worth the knowing here on earth,
among its weather-decked hills, its beasts and birds
in their ceaseless cycles, migrations. Of course the glorious earth

will take me back, of course the young-year hare give profligate birth.

Acknowledgments:

All poems here, aside from a few sections from "Birds, a Farrago," have earlier appeared—sometimes in slightly, or even considerably different forms—in periodicals; I am grateful to their editors and staffs:

AGNI Review, Ascent, The Atlantic Monthly, The Christian Century, Cold Mountain Review, The Georgia Review, Green Mountains Review, The Harvard Review, The Hudson Review, Hunger Mountain, The Journal, Margie, New Ohio Review, Salmagundi, Shenandoah, The Southern Review, Tar River Poetry, and *The Yale Review.*

I want also to acknowledge the abiding friendship of Stephen Arkin, Fleda Brown, Jill Rosser and Marjan Strojan, so helpful to me in completing these poems, even when they didn't know it—and so sustaining in countless other ways. As over and over, of course, are my wondrous wife Robin and all five children.

Sydney Lea has published eight prior volumes of poetry. His 2000 book, *Pursuit of a Wound*, was a Pulitzer finalist, and the collection before that, *To the Bone*, was co-winner of The Poets' Prize. Founder and longtime editor of *New England Review*, Lea has also published the novel *A Place in Mind* and two naturalist nonfiction titles, *Hunting the Whole Way Home* and *A Little Wildness*. He has received fellowships from the Fulbright, Guggenheim, and Rockefeller Foundations, and has taught at Dartmouth, Middlebury, Wesleyan, and Yale, as well as at several European universities. Active in conservation and literacy advocacy, he lives in Vermont.